RIVER
ADVENTURES

THAMES

D0552559

W
FRANKLIN WATTS
LONDON • SYDNEY

◀ At this treatment works, wastewater from homes and factories is decontaminated before being fed back into the river.

Lakes and reservoirs

At Staines, the Thames heads south, criss-crossing under roads and motorways and weaving among lakes and reservoirs.

As well as being a place for recreation and a transport route, the river is a vital source of water for London. Every day, millions of litres of water from the Thames are diverted to lakes and reservoirs. Water is then pumped to treatment works, to be cleaned and filtered before being piped to people's homes.

Who needs water?

Roughly 79 per cent of London's water is used in people's homes. The rest is used by industries, including breweries and paper-makers. Some of the biggest users are power stations like the one at Didcot in Berkshire, where Thames water is used to cool the giant electricity turbines.

▶ At a Thames Water laboratory, a scientist examines a water sample to make sure it is clean and safe to drink.

Leabharlanna Poibli Chathair Baile Átha Cliath
Dublin City Public Libraries

YOU ARE HERE

River Thames
Kew
Richmond
Hampton
Teddington
Kingston
Hampton Court

The Tidal Thames

At Teddington Lock, you reach an important stage in your journey. Here, fresh water meets salt water carried in from the sea. From now on, the Thames is a tidal river.

▼ Teddington Weir marks the start of the tidal section of the Thames, known as the Tideway.

The tide effect

Although the sea is nearly 104 km (65 miles) away, the tide has a big effect on the river. Instead of flowing steadily out towards the sea, the fresh water heading downstream is pushed back by the incoming tide. Depending on the strength of the tide, the water that flows over Teddington Weir can take anything from three weeks to three months to reach the sea.

▶ Hampton Court was well connected to London by river. Over the palace gate, a clock still shows the time of high tide at London Bridge.

Parks and palaces

Between Hampton and Kew, the river is famous for its stately homes and royal parks and palaces. Many of these sites were chosen because of their riverside location.

Hampton Court was the favourite palace of Henry VIII. Kings, queens and important people often travelled this stretch of the river in royal barges. Travelling with the tide made the journey much quicker, so trips up and downriver were carefully timed.

Controlling the tide

At Richmond, a very low tide could mean that the river was little more than a shallow stream. Under this bridge, a barrage has been built with gates which can be raised and lowered. This protects boats moored upstream from running aground when the tide goes out.

◀ The barrage at Richmond helps to control the effect of the tide.

The Working River

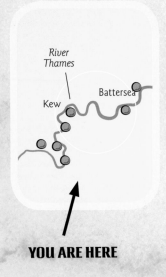

YOU ARE HERE

After the green spaces of Richmond and Kew, you are now in urban West London. Here, the river is lined with offices, flats, warehouses and industrial buildings.

A transport route

In the past, the river was a vital transport route. Many industries were based along its banks, and ships and barges carried supplies of coal and other raw materials which were unloaded at wharves on the waterfront.

▼ *Battersea Power Station once produced electricity for the whole of London, but has been disused since 1982. Coal was brought by river every day and unloaded by cranes which still stand on the waterfront.*

◀ Barges towed by tugboats were once a common sight on the river. Today, most heavy goods are carried by road or rail.

As London grew, road and rail transport gradually took over from boats, and use of the river declined. Today, a few working boats can be seen, but most of the traffic on the river is made up of tourist or pleasure boats.

Bridges and tunnels

Until the 18th century, London Bridge was the only place in London where the river could be crossed. Today, there are 33 bridges across the Thames between Hampton and Southwark. Pedestrian and rail tunnels have also been built underneath the Thames, and there are road tunnels at Blackwall, Rotherhithe and Dartford.

Commuting by river

Riverbus is a good way to travel this stretch of the Thames. There are no traffic jams, and you can enjoy some of the best views of London from the river. More than 2,000 commuters a day now travel to work on the Thames. Catching a riverbus is as easy as catching a bus or underground train.

Leabharlann na Cabraí
Cabra Library
Tel: 8691414

Westminster

River
Thames
Westminster

Battersea

YOU ARE HERE

At Westminster, your boat ride takes you past some of London's most historic buildings. Since 1066, 38 English kings and queens have been crowned in Westminster Abbey, and laws have been debated in the Houses of Parliament since the 13th century.

▼ The Houses of Parliament overlook the Thames at Westminster.

▶ The Millennium Footbridge connects the South Bank with St Paul's Cathedral. It is the newest bridge over the Thames.

The Embankment

The Thames here flows between high stone walls called embankments. These were built in Victorian times to protect the city from flooding. Before this, the river was flanked on either side by muddy land. Much of London's sewage ended up here, and many Londoners died from diseases caused by drinking water from the river.

The London Eye

On the north bank, the Victoria Embankment carries a steady stream of traffic east and west through the city. On the other side of the river is the giant ferris wheel known as the London Eye. From the top of this, you have a far-reaching view of the Thames as it flows through London.

▶ London's embankments and sewers were built by Joseph Bazalgette (1819–91). His memorial stands on the Victoria Embankment.

The 'Great Stink'

During a heatwave in 1858, the smell of sewage in the Thames became so bad that Parliament had to be suspended. Afterwards, the government decided to build a huge new system of tunnels to get rid of the city's waste. The new sewers stopped drinking water from being contaminated by sewage. This saved the lives of thousands of Londoners.

FLVM'N' VINC'LA P°SV'T

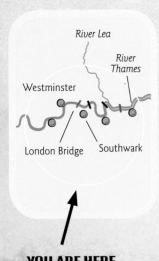

YOU ARE HERE

The Port of London

A river crossing has existed on the site of London Bridge since Roman times. It was here that London began, as a tiny settlement on the banks of the Thames.

▼ *The earliest crossing at London Bridge was built of wood. The present stone bridge dates from 1973. It leads directly to the City of London financial district.*

An ancient crossing

The first bridge over the Thames was built by the Romans in around 50 CE. The Romans chose the site carefully: it was the furthest point inland where seagoing ships could anchor in the tidal waters of the Thames. On the river banks, a port was built where goods could be unloaded, and the Roman town of Londinium grew up around it.

River trade

The river has brought wealth to London ever since. In the 18th and 19th centuries, London was the busiest port in the world. There were so many vessels on the Thames, it was said that you could cross the river by stepping from one ship to the next!

The growth of the docks

The original Port of London was based between London Bridge and Wapping. As trade increased, shipping companies built their own docks further downstream. The last to be built was King George V dock, in 1921.

▲ Tower Bridge at the entrance to the old Port of London has sections of road called bascules. These can be raised to let tall ships through.

The Thames Tunnel

The Thames Tunnel at Rotherhithe was the world's first underwater tunnel. It was built by the engineer Isambard Kingdom Brunel and his father Mark Isambard Brunel between 1825 and 1843. Digging under the riverbed was highly dangerous, and there were often floods when the roof collapsed, and mud and water poured in.

Docklands

As you head east from Tower Bridge, you can see a cluster of high-rise blocks ahead of you. These are the giant towers of London's Docklands.

River Lea

Rotherhithe Tunnel

Blackwall Tunnel

Westminster

Greenwich

Docklands

River Thames

YOU ARE HERE

▼ *The business and financial district at Canary Wharf is the heart of modern Docklands. Around 90,000 people work here.*

The end of the docks

Over the last 30 years this area has changed a lot. In the 1960s, the London docks began to close down one by one, as trade shifted to bigger ports near the sea. Within a few years the docks had become a derelict wasteland.

In the 1980s, a huge building project transformed the old warehouses and wharves into new riverside communities. Smart new flats and offices were built around the dock basins. By 1998, more than 24,000 new homes had been built, and 2,700 new businesses had moved into the area.

A naval town

At Greenwich, you break your journey to visit the National Maritime Museum and Royal Observatory. On display are the famous Harrison Clocks that first allowed sailors to plot their position accurately on long sea voyages. Greenwich is also the home of the *Cutty Sark*, a great tall-masted sailing ship that once raced to bring back cargoes of tea from China.

Policing the Thames

Since 1800, crime-fighting on the river has been the job of the Thames River Police. In the past, smuggling was common, and cargo ships on the Thames were often a target for river pirates. Today, police launches are more likely to be on the lookout for drug-runners and people-traffickers.

▶ Tourist boats and riverbuses bring visitors to the old Royal Naval College at Greenwich.

The Thames Barrier

Around the site of the O2 Arena at Greenwich, the river turns a tight loop. Ahead of you now are the giant piers of the Thames Barrier.

Queen Elizabeth II
Road Bridge

Thames
Barrier

Woolwich

Greenwich

M25
Ringroad

Dartford
Tunnel

YOU ARE HERE

▼ *East of London, the landscape is flat and low-lying. Many industries are based here. This part of the river was once badly polluted by chemicals and other waste.*

The Thames Barrier

The Thames Barrier has been in place since 1984. It is London's main defence against flooding. Between the piers are huge curved gates below the water. Normally the gates are lowered to allow ships to pass through. When the flood risk is high, the gates are raised to hold back the tide.

◄ The Thames Barrier spans a 520-m (1,706-ft) wide section of the Thames at Woolwich.

The Thames Barrier is only part of London's flood defences. There are 36 other, smaller barriers, and more than 185 km (115 miles) of defence walls along the riverbanks. On average, the Thames Barrier closes three times a year to protect London from surge tides from the sea. Luckily, no high storm tides are forecast today, so you can continue safely on your way.

What is a surge tide?

When storms at sea coincide with high tides, a surge tide can sweep upriver, causing flooding and widespread destruction. London is at risk because much of the land on which it is built is low-lying. Experts say the city is sinking at a rate of 30 cm (12 in) every 100 years.

► The Queen Elizabeth II road bridge crosses the river at Dartford. The height of the bridge allows cruise ships to pass under it on their way to the Port of London.

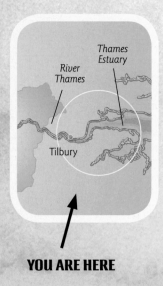

YOU ARE HERE

The Thames Estuary

As the Thames flows out towards the sea, it opens out into a broad expanse of mudflats and salt marshes. Your river journey is nearly over.

A shipping route

This part of the Thames is a busy route for oil tankers, container ships, bulk carriers and ferries. The river is wide and slow-moving at this point. Parts of it are flanked by wide banks called levées which protect the land on either side from flooding.

▼ Egypt Bay on the Thames Estuary was once a favourite spot for smugglers bringing stolen goods ashore.

Tilbury

In ancient times, Tilbury was important in defending the river from enemy ships and preventing attacks on London. Today, Tilbury Docks is one of the busiest ports in the UK, handling passenger ships and container vessels from all over the world.

▲ A container ship heads up the estuary towards Tilbury Docks.

The future

As London continues to grow, the future of the Thames Estuary is uncertain. With the completion of the high-speed Channel Tunnel Rail Link, the region is set to become a centre for new jobs and housing. London's fourth airport may be located here too.

New development will certainly bring wealth, but many are concerned about the impact on wildlife, especially the many wading birds that live in the area.

Thames barges

Thames barges were perfect for sailing the shallow waters of the Thames Estuary, and restored barges still sail the river today. Built of wood with huge sails, the barges were originally used to transport bricks, sand, coal and grain. Over time, they were gradually replaced by steam-powered vessels.

Leabharlanna Poibli Chathair Baile Átha Cliath
Dublin City Public Libraries

Glossary

arable farming growing crops in a field

barrage a barrier to halt or reduce the flow of a river

cholera a deadly disease spread by dirty water

commuter a person who travels to work by car, bus or train

container ship a ship that transports goods in steel crates

course the route followed by a river

decline to reduce or become less

decontaminate to clean or remove impurities from something

derelict abandoned and run-down

embankment a high wall used to contain the flow of a river

erosion the gradual wearing away of soil or rock

fertile good for growing

ford a place where a river is shallow and can be crossed

gorge a deep river valley with steep rocky sides

Ice Age a time long ago when the temperature dropped and the Earth was covered with ice

lock a device for lifting or lowering boats from one level of water to another

minnow a tiny fish that lives in shallow water

Norman Conquest the time from 1066 onwards when Britain was conquered by the Normans

pedestrian a person who travels on foot

polluted made dirty, e.g. by sewage

reservoir a lake used to store water

salt marsh an area of muddy land in a coastal area

scholar a person who spends their time studying

settlement a place where people live permanently

source the beginning of a river, usually a lake or spring

suspended cancelled or abandoned

tideway the part of a river that is affected by tides

tributary a stream or river that flows into another, bigger one

turbine a wheel that is turned by water to produce electricity

urban belonging to a town or city

wastewater water that has been washed down a drain

water meadow a field that is partly flooded at certain times of year

weir a type of dam used to control the flow of a river

wharf (*pl.* **wharves**) a place beside a river where goods are unloaded

Thames Quiz*

Find the answers in this book, or look them up online.

1 Match the captions to the pictures.

1

2

3

4

5

6

A The London Eye

B A pier of the Thames Barrier at Woolwich

C The statue of the Sphinx on the Victoria Embankment

D A deer in Windsor Great Park

E Punting on the river at Oxford

F The statue of 'Old Father Thames' at Lechlade Lock

2 These places can all be found along the Thames. Put them in the right order, starting with the ones nearest to the sea:

Windsor
Hampton Court
Tilbury Docks
Abingdon
Lechlade
Battersea

3 True or false?

'The Thames was once a tributary of the River Rhine that flows through Germany.'

4 This bronze head is on display in the British Museum. Do you know who it represents, and where it was found?

*Answers on page 32.

Websites and Further Reading

Websites

- www.primaryhomeworkhelp.co.uk/riverthames
  A detailed and well-illustrated virtual journey down the Thames.
- www.museumoflondon.org.uk/explore-online/pocket-histories/
  Interesting information about the history of the river, and London.

Further Reading

Rivers (The Geography Detective Investigates series), Jen Green (Wayland, 2006)

River (Your Local Area series), Ruth Thomson (Wayland, 2010)

Index

Answers to Thames Quiz

1 1D, 2F, 3C, 4E, 5A, 6B. **2** Tilbury Docks, Battersea, Hampton Court, Windsor, Abingdon, Lechlade. **3** True. Before Britain was separated from continental Europe, the two rivers met in the area now covered by southern North Sea. **4** The bronze head is part of a statue of the Roman Emperor Hadrian. It was found buried in the mud below London Bridge in 1834.